W9-CMU-956

NOW THAT I KNOW

WHICH SIDE IS UP

NOW THAT I KNOW WHICH SIDE IS UP

ELI DJEDDAH

Now That I Know Which Side Is Up
is published by
TEN SPEED PRESS
900 Modoc
Berkeley, California 94706

© 1976 Institute For Personal Development, Inc.

You may order single copies prepaid direct
from the publisher for $3.95 plus $.50 per
copy postage and handling.

ISBN 0-913668-44-3
Second printing
Printed in the United States of America

Acknowledgment is gratefully made
to Jennifer Cross for her advice, assistance
and contribution in the writing of this book.

To my wife, Rona, whose insight and patience made this book possible.

CONTENTS

1

INTRODUCTION

Most of us, if we are honest about it, would like to be able to persuade other people to do what *we* want. Not only success, but much of our own happiness is inextricably linked to our relations with these other people. We need them to pay us more attention, to appreciate our inner beauty, our brains, talents, goodness, even our warts. Deep inside us there is still the little child who clamors for attention the easy way, who would like to push buttons that could evoke predictably favorable responses.

This can be done, because the "buttons" are nothing less than eternal principles of human behavior, based on people's social conditioning and their deepest emotional needs for love and security.

These principles are constant, but their application has both a positive and a negative side. If you understand what you are doing, and are socially constructive, you can obtain automatically good responses from most people most of the time, because you have pushed the button which satisfies their needs. In short, you will be right side up. But push a button inadvertently, or with the wrong purpose, and you may get the shaft. Sooner or later we all must decide which way it is going to be.

The majority of us remain amateurs at persuasion, although we could do both ourselves and society a favor by getting better at it. Most of our daily button pushing is done at an unconscious level, and we are lucky that it is often harmless, even ritualistic, what Transactional Analysis calls "stroking." But we con-

stantly stumble on many other ways to evoke
pain, pleasure or a mixture of both.

Think how *you* respond to these triggers: the
sound of your name, a child crying, a tune, a
special place, a certain smell or perfume.
Think also of the many techniques we all use
to try to get what we want. A young child cries
or wheedles its mother. Lovers kiss and touch.
A housewife talks her husband into doing the
dishes, or the repairman into hurrying round
to fix the TV.

Unfortunately, our persuasions also have
their ugly side. We nag, whine, sulk or lose our
temper. Problem emotions and situations
press buttons in ourselves and others. We
offend people, get sick, have migraines, upset
stomachs and bitter, senseless family quarrels.
Alas, our rational mind does not necessarily
know or approve of what the nasty child in us
is doing. We are pushing buttons all right, but
they are the wrong ones, and often we are
pushing them for the wrong reasons.

As a result, we crave love and affection

without knowing how to get enough to satisfy us. If we are lucky, we can transmute our longings into art, power or money. More often, our frustration leads us to petty revenges which sabotage some of the finest aspects of our humanity. We push people away, we cripple, even destroy them. They repay us in kind, setting off a vicious cycle of loneliness and unhappiness.

Sooner or later we encounter other stresses that tax our social skills to the breaking point, or beyond. We discover inequality, injustice and race or sex prejudice. We marry, live in little boxes and when the claustrophobia of nuclear family life wears us down, we split, leaving another generation of children with a bitter inheritance of hurt and insecurity. Even if our family survives, we gypsy around the country in search of promotion, or even peace and quiet, and thereby saddle ourselves with the perpetual, often wearying challenge of growing new roots.

Silent victims of our struggle are every-where—establishment dropouts, lonely corporate wives quieting their discontent with booze or Valium, emotional clamshells, bull-shitters and overall an almost tangible miasma of apathy and depression.

The corporate world, for all its rewards and excitements, compounds our problems. Despite a growing awareness of the need for good human relations, business life often makes them impossible. We are forced to suppress our emotions in the name of rationality and efficiency, and the price of "success" is too often a kind of mutilation, of which we may not be completely aware. Running to bureaucracy or academia is not necessarily the answer. The rules may be slightly different, but the game and the payoff are much the same.

In business, inability to get along with others is more of a handicap than lack of brains or talent. All the merit and education in the world are meaningless in isolation; they only have true significance in relation to other people.

Over the years I have counseled hundreds of executives. Many of them were extremely able, but at least eight out of every ten were

handicapped by some human relations problems, both at work and at home, with the one
reinforcing the other.

These problems can be helped, even avoided.
Anyone can understand people and communicate better, not just as an academic exercise, or to play emotional striptease, but to get
full value from life membership in the human
race. This should not require professional
counseling. In fact, the study of people is too
important to be left to gurus, psychiatrists or
other experts. It is the daily, lifelong concern of
everyone.

Now That I Know Which Side is Up is an attempt to help you through the maze of human
relations. It is a practical philosophy which was
developed by observing life here in America,
Europe and the Middle East, and shaped by
my counseling career in this country.

Here you will find a series of very important
principles of behavior, the "buttons" which
move people to action and reaction. Individ-
ually these are not new. They are the time-
less, universal truths that we humans have

16

discovered about ourselves. I hope that when you see them again they will strike you with a stark realism they did not have before. Also, I have put them together in a new way, which will give you very powerful tools to improve yourself and your situation. These principles work. They have been tested in my own life, and in the lives of those I have counseled.

What can this book do for *you*? Assuming you are not seriously emotionally disturbed, it can give you a new and deeper understanding of yourself and other people. This understanding will make you attractive, whatever your physical appearance. You will have the kind of inner beauty which is an important ingredient of charisma. You will also have a new sense of yourself which is more valuable than anything money can buy.

What is done with these gifts obviously depends on you. Almost certainly you will get more positive feedback from other people, which will make you more able to love yourself, replacing your doubt and pain with silent, unexpressed self-acceptance and lived-out joy.

Being loved, and loveable, will reinforce your desire and ability to repay in kind. The result will be a warm, powerful wave which will actually push you still farther towards the satisfaction of your own needs for love, approval and—however you care to define it—happiness and success. You will also be more skillful at handling problem people and situations, particularly those difficulties stemming from lack of understanding and poor communications.

The kind of changes you can get from this book are not painful, provided you do not brood over past mistakes. But they *do* require an open mind, concentration and willingness to work. The greater your need, the more profound will be your sense of illumination.

In the end you cannot beat the human race, only join it, learn to live with it and love it so that it will love you back. This book contains the principles that show you how and why. Each chapter also contains exercises to use in your daily life, to prove the principles (even improve on them) and to check your progress. You might read the book through first, then go back and spend several weeks on each chapter and its exer-

18

cises. Try to do these with someone close to you, to get sensitive and honest feedback about the reality of your expectations and your growing skills. But above all, please do them! Nobody learns by reading alone, or by listening to good advice. If we did, we should all be unbelievably, perhaps unbearably wise. In reality, we have to agree with John Keats: "Nothing becomes real till it is experienced —even a proverb is no proverb to you till your life has illustrated it."

PRINCIPLES

In the end you cannot beat the human race, only join it, learn to live with it and love it so that it will love you back.

EXERCISES

1. Start a diary or notebook to accompany these exercises. Use it to record your thoughts, feelings and progress.

2. Make a list of the ways you use to try to:
   (a) get attention
   (b) get approval
   (c) try to influence the people in your life
       —particularly your boss, employees, partner and children. How aware are you of what you are doing? How effective are you? (Cross check with your partner.) What are you *not* getting that you want?

2

AFFIRMATIONS

For everything there is a season and a time
for every purpose under heaven:
A time to be born, and a time to die;
A time to plant, and a time to pluck up what
is planted;
A time to kill, and a time to heal;
A time to break down, and a time to
build up;
A time to weep, and a time to laugh;
A time to mourn, and a time to dance;
A time to cast away stones, and a time to
gather stones together;

A time to embrace, and a time to refrain
from embracing;
   A time to seek, and a time to lose;
   A time to keep, and a time to cast away;
   A time to rend, and a time to sew;
   A time to keep silence, and a time to speak;
   A time to love, and a time to hate;
   A time for war and a time for peace.

Ecclesiastes

We might add to Ecclesiastes; a time to reflect, and a time to act. At best, the unexamined life is hardly worth living; and there are times of crisis when our need for reflection is more urgent and necessary than the need for action. We have to wrench ourselves away from the more or less unthinking pursuit of our usual routines into a rediscovery of what life, in particular our life, is all about.

People have been doing this since time immemorial, long before Descartes took refuge from war and winter by a big stove and opened his personal search with the unforgettable statement: "Cogito, ergo sum," I think, therefore I am. Centuries earlier, Aristotle wrote in his *Ethics*: "A knowledge of the good is a great advantage to us in the conduct of our lives. Are we not more likely to hit the mark if we have a target?"

Very often our return to first principles is motivated by being in deep water. We are out of work, experiencing marital trouble, lonely or simply frightened and confused. Our lives have started on a downward trend, and we think poorly of ourselves, and therefore of others. In our worst moments we conclude that life is a shuck and that people are no damn good.

Sometimes the mere ticking of our internal biological clock is enough to trigger the process—the storms of adolescence, the anxiety of middle age, and later on, our reluctant but inevitable confrontation with aging and death.

We should start with the premise that *the purpose of all life is the affirmation of life.* We cannot, of course, deny the existence of death, or as Freud and others believe, the death-wish present in all living things, and the sometimes unbearable tension between these two forces.

23

Maybe in the end the whole universe will self-destruct, but meanwhile life has been programmed to win.

This instinct for survival is illustrated by our great powers of self-healing. You cut your finger; in a few days there will be hardly a mark. Perhaps you can think yourself out of a headache. Your sick dog or cat will creep off to eat certain plants or grasses. You prune a tree or bush, and it will grow more vigorously.

Mankind as a whole shows a tremendous drive to survive, and to choose spiritual and social affirmations. Though the balance is often precarious, we seek light rather than darkness, life rather than death and peace rather than war. We all enjoy love, sex and food. We prefer weddings to funerals, marriage to divorce, Christmas to Ash Wednesday or Channukah to Yom Kippur. Whatever our taste in beauty, we delight in laughter, a running child, flowers, dawns and sunsets. Whatever our religious beliefs, we all to some degree fear darkness, disease, death and uncertainty.

Philosophically, our quest for affirmation

has been expressed in ways ranging from a belief in reincarnation to the search for salvation or a perfect good. A more familiar idea is the pain and pleasure principle, the first principle of human relations. Simply put, *we can always be counted on to choose what is favorable to us and reject the unfavorable.* What we choose may or may not be "good," pleasant or easy, but it always supports what we perceive to be our lifestyle.

We are so programmed—and so, for that matter, are animals and plants—that we store memories of old pains and pleasures, developing an almost Pavlovian reflex towards associated events or circumstances. A dog will salivate at the sound of the bell which means dinner; children go wild with anticipation at Christmas or Halloween. A toddler who has been burned will shy away from heat; many people similarly shy away from their mothers-in-law.

Most of us have a well trained instinct for avoiding painful or unfavorable things and people. Meeting someone for the first time, our senses are alert; is this person *for* me or *against* me, will he help or hinder me, is he pleasant to be around? If the answers are negative, or if we sense rapacity or failure, a curtain comes down—we do not want to know more.

Society as a whole turns away from people who are cruel or predatory at the expense of others, even when they appear successful. We lock them in jail, ruin or ostracize them. We shrug to hear that a bullet or heart attack has felled them one dark night. We also turn away from the leper, the beggar, the bum, the bore, anyone whose misery or need makes more demands on us than we can meet, or whose plight we would hate to share.

We also, unfortunately, cold shoulder those who cannot produce, or who have no future prospect of doing so; which accounts for our inhumanity to the poor, elderly and chronically sick. And our callousness is mirrored in nature by the exacting accountant who strips off withered leaves, fells dead trees and kills the drones once their usefulness is ended. It is the same within our own bodies. The message

26

is clear: *Affirm life in one way or another—or get cut off.*

This duty lies behind every lasting code of ethics mankind has ever devised, which in turn is supported by every major legal system. Truly ethical behavior is that which, to the best of our intentions, knowledge and beliefs, will affirm life to the greatest degree, starting with ourselves and those around us. Practically speaking, we should try to do the greatest good for the greatest number over the longest period.

The dark side of this coin is rejection—to be cut off from our tribe. So powerful is our need to join humanity and get its continuing approval, that we are all ultrasensitive to even the faintest whisper of rejection, and insecure because of this. Each rejection is a taste of dying, and a pain we should never inflict on others, or they on us.

Sooner or later, we must all decide if we are *for* life, against it or merely doing time. It is a question which becomes critical when we are troubled or depressed or living out a stalemate.

How much of what you are doing and being is life-affirming—or have you fallen into the trap of other people's demands or expectations? Are you doing, being or experiencing enough things which make you feel good? How could you do more? What are your short and long-term goals, and do they really reflect your best interests?

It helps to write a short autobiography, stressing everything you have done, felt or been in your life that gave you the feeling of greatest accomplishment. You might be shocked to discover how long it has been since anything you did seemed really worthwhile. More likely, you will discover a distinct pattern in your achievements.

One man's autobiography showed that he had consistently abandoned people and situations when the going got rough—tantamount to getting off the train before it stops. Not only had this created a huge amount of extra work, he also saddled himself with the pain and rejection of a sequence of new beginnings, when a little more patience and one more push

would have made him successful in whatever
he did.

You will also benefit from a fresh look at
your goals and values. Many people believe
they want to be rich, but discover that what
really moves them is their need for love, recognition or simply to serve others. No wonder
that as many as eighty percent of us are in the
wrong work! Obviously, if love *is* what you
desire, you will not get it by chasing after a
bigger salary, any more than you will get
recognition by holing up in a cave or a lonely
farm out in the boondocks.

Even more important, how do you feel about
yourself? It is almost impossible to begin
changing your life, or to be hopeful and positive, if you feel badly about yourself.

*Each of us has an obligation, both to ourselves and
humanity, to be perfectly fit—physically, mentally and
spiritually.* Until this is true, we can hardly do
our best in human relations, communications
or any other area. If you are physically fit,
everyone who meets you will take joy in the
dynamic expression of life you represent, and

reflect it back. If you are mentally balanced, everyone will respect and be drawn to your confidence and alertness. If you are spiritually fit, everyone will sense an inner strength and integrity, even though many won't be able to pinpoint its source.

Our need to cultivate personal beauty should not be confused with vanity. Given the constrained lives most of us lead, it is a struggle for everyone to keep physically fit. Many of us are underexercised and overweight, with a certain lackluster flabbiness which speaks of tension and self-neglect. Flesh and spirit are woefully out of shape; both our bodies and the aura we project reflect this. At any committee meeting, party or even on a crowded street, the impression we make is so negative we repel those we would join. Do you sometimes feel like this?

We also need from time to time to come to grips with our emotional problems, with or without professional counseling. Most of us carry a load of skeletons in our psychic closets.

We wear a hair shirt or we are afraid of success or we cannot forgive our parents for the real or imagined wrongs they did us. The prospect of happiness makes us guilty or uneasy; yet happiness is the ultimate affirmation. We have signed no contract with life to be miserable.

Getting back into shape is much easier if you do not have to do it alone, but have the active cooperation of a partner. Because *the comfort of words is not enough; they must be backed by sympathy and the power of good example.* A wife, husband or friend needs to employ creative listening; listening that empathizes with pain and problems, that encourages one towards a solution by directed questioning, coupled with enthusiasm for the responses. Each one must realize how deeply the other is troubled, and come to terms with any feelings of anger and disappointment. These helpers can also take an active lead in the healing process, reinforcing their partner's good intentions by their own good examples. If one decides to go on a diet, into therapy, take up jogging, do new things or make new friends, the other should join in wholeheartedly, using the powerful tool of example by doing.

The quest for personal beauty is often the best way to start a new, positive trend in your life. The wise Chinese proverb says: "The longest journey begins with the first step." So long as you have the right purpose as a goal, it does not matter what this step is, or how small it may be.

Once you have taken this step, you can then utilize another very important human relations principle: *We need to complete anything we start.* Of course, we all know the person whose life is littered with new beginnings and unfinished projects. But in general, this need to complete amounts to a near compulsion—even though what we have started may not be in our best interests. What we are doing or saying has a certain inevitability, whether it is a job to be done at dinner time, or that unforgiveable remark which slips out during a family quarrel even though we know it is wrong.

This need to complete is dinned into us from

early childhood. We are taught to eat *all* the food on our plates, put away *all* our toys, and wash behind our ears. In this way we are educated to expect perfection. Of course we can never completely achieve it, and the gap points a relentless finger of dissatisfaction.

Take the first positive step, and your ego will be on the line. You *have* to finish. Better still, tell all your friends about it. You will discover another important human relations concept, *the power of social approval.*

A friend of mine accidentally found this out when he announced that he might cycle from London to Yugoslavia. At first, he had no serious intention of going, but after the umpteenth person said: "What, haven't you gone *yet?*" he unpacked his 10-speed and left. However, you do not have to cycle that far to prove the point. Just start a new hobby or go on a diet and you will sell your friends on it with all the missionary zeal of an ex-alcoholic.

Pursuing new activities will suggest other ways to change your life. One is to form new habits which will economize on your energy, and exercise your self-discipline. Your friends will almost certainly respond; if not, you should think about making new ones. Adding to or changing your circle will produce more good vibrations, fresh examples and a renewed commitment to the power of social approval.

Another way to use the power of social approval is through those rituals developed over the centuries by people seeking love and its expression—etiquette, thoughtfulness, music, art, generosity, remembrance, kindness, sympathy for the pain of others. When these stem from a genuine concern for humanity, they are a true expression of beauty, and one which invokes the most fundamental principle of human relations, that of *reciprocity*, without which no society can function.

Most of us think of reciprocity in terms of the Biblical phrase: "An eye for an eye and a tooth for a tooth." But this is incomplete. To it should be added: "A rose for a rose, and a kiss for a kiss."

The true law of reciprocity is: "As you are to

me, so am I to you." The Book of Proverbs says: "As a face in water answereth to face, heart answereth to heart in man." You come to me friendly, with your lips and heart, and I respond. There is very little choice about my response. I must be friendly also, with my lips and heart. You say: "Good morning!" in the elevator and I can do no less than smile back. You praise my appearance and I can do no less than give you my heart. You do me a favor and you have pushed a powerful button which obliges me to repay you in kind.

A scientist who was somewhat skeptical of this whole idea of reciprocity devised a little experiment to test it out. When some neighborhood children came to play in his yard, he rudely ordered them to leave. As they ran off, they jeered back at him, throwing sticks and leaves they had wrenched from one of his trees. The next day he saw them again, and they were about to scuttle by on the other side of the road. He called one over: "Hey, Johnny! Look at this cart I'm making for my kid. Come

and give me your advice about it." In a flash all
the children swarmed around, helping, criti-
cizing, telling him about their own projects.
The ogre had suddenly become their friend,
and the bad scene was forgotten.

Over the long term, reciprocity leads us to
pay and pay back situations, both good and
bad, which will be discussed in another chapter. But in the short run, you can profitably
use this principle to create friendly feelings
in people who live in a twilight zone of being
taken for granted, or simply never being
thanked. Many service workers resent being
treated as less than human, or garbage cans for
our complaints. How long is it since you smiled
or thanked or started a friendly conversation
with a harrassed waitress, a ticket clerk or a
supermarket checker? How long is it since you
helped your kids with their homework or a pet
project or told your partner how handsome,
sexy or gorgeous he or she looks? Do you remember other people's birthdays, not just
your family's, but your secretary's, and your

friends'? And do you thank people for helping you—not just for obvious favors, but for a dinner party, a business lunch, even for giving you a good job interview? You will surely find the harvest of goodwill ten times worth the tiny effort of time and remembrance.

PRINCIPLES

The purpose of life is the affirmation of life.

Affirm life in one way or another or get cut off.

We can always be counted on to choose what is favorable to us and reject the unfavorable.

We need to complete anything we start.

Personal beauty is an obligation, both to ourselves and humanity.

To change ourselves, we need the sympathetic ear and good example of someone close to us, and the social approval of those around us.

The true law of reciprocity is: As you are to me, so am I to you.

EXERCISES

1. Self-evaluation.
    (a) List in your diary or notebook the things you do which you enjoy and which are life-affirming. Now those which are boring or painful. What can you do to reverse the balance?
    (b) Write your own thoughts on: What do I believe in? What is the purpose of life?
    (c) What are your goals, now and for the future? Are they the proper ones for you?
    (d) What are the major achievements of your life? Do they fall into any particular pattern?
    (e) Do you enjoy your work? If not, should you change jobs, or, if you are at home, should you try to get a job or continue your education? How much time do you want to spend working, how much with your family? How much money do you and your family *really* need to enjoy life?

(f) Do you need to lose weight? Start by seeing a doctor, then count calories. Choose a sensible diet and stick with it. Eat less of *everything*, particularly starches and fats. If you drink alcohol, try to cut down. Check your weight at the start, and continue to record your weight loss.

(g) Do you need more exercise? If nothing else, do 10 minutes a day of the Royal Canadian Air Force Exercises appropriate to your age and sex.

(h) Look in the mirror—and get someone else to help you look. Check your expression and the way you walk. Is it habitually joyous, depressed, blank, suspicious? Is your voice cheerful or flat? How do you greet your partner and children in the morning, or returning from work? How do you walk into your office, greet your colleagues or students, answer the phone? Act these things out. How can you be more affirmative?

2. Practice affirmation.
   (a) Make a list of all the rituals you can think of which people have developed to give and receive love and consideration. For example: Letters of condolence, birthday greetings, or a simple: "Hello, how are you?"
   (b) How many of these have you done lately?
   (c) Do something new which is life-affirming; e.g. cook a gourmet meal, bring your wife flowers, your husband coffee in bed. Make or build something. Volunteer help for a good cause, organization or group.

3. What your partner can do.
   (a) Listen sympathetically to your mate or friend's problems—but don't make listening a substitute for action.
   (b) Help the other person with self-evaluation.
   (c) Surprise him or her with an act of love and affirmation.

(d) Get yourself in good physical shape too.

(e) Take a lead in starting new activities.

(f) Are you feeling angry with, or disappointed in the other person? Can you carefully pick a good moment for an *adult* discussion of these problems?

4. On rising each day think of a loved one and let the thought color your day.

3

JEHOVAH AND THE ANGEL: A DISCUSSION OF EVERYONE'S FAVORITE COMPLEXES

Do unto others as you would have them do unto you.
This universal advice has been found in the
teachings of every major religion and in the
philosophy of every group founded to further
mankind. It is the core of the important principle of reciprocity; simple, effective—and if
only we could do it, our human relations

problems would evaporate like morning dew. Needless to say, most of us can't.

The biggest stumbling block is our *Jehovah complex*. Whatever our sex, age or condition, to ourselves *we are in a real sense the center of the universe*. The world begins for us when we open our eyes on the delivery table. We are entirely self-centered, and our raucous cry for food and attention contains godlike rage if mommy is late or the service poor. Even as toddlers, when our divinity has been eroded by such reminders of mortality as weaning and learning to walk, we still secretly believe in our terrible powers. It is a shock to realize we cannot make the rain go away simply by shouting, or that our parents do not fall on the floor when we scream out our anger. Of course, we grow up, more or less. But we never entirely escape the reality of being confined to one body, looking out through one set of eyes and being overwhelmed from time to time by our feelings. All things begin and end with *me*, until I close my eyes for the last time, and the world itself ends.

Allied to this is our *Angel complex: Everything we do has to be right.* A classic example of this concerns the burning of the libraries of Alexandria, one of the glories of the ancient world. When asked why he wanted to destroy the accumulation of wisdom, the Caliph Omar is said to have replied. "Do you not understand that either they approve us or they disapprove us? Approval is redundant, disapproval is sin. Burn them."

Being right is not a feeling confined to the high and mighty. Nor does it have anything to do with ethics, or even good sense. Years ago, a woman shot and killed her husband at the bridge table because his game was lousy. More recently, a Frenchman disposed of two wives because he couldn't stand their cooking. Both were *right* in the sense that what they did seemed inevitable and proper. In addition, the woman had probably built her whole life around playing bridge and the Frenchman on being a gourmet.

One day when I was having dinner next to the warden of the local jail, I asked him how many inmates he had, and how many were guilty? He laughed. "We've got about five thousand," he said, "but not a single one of them is guilty." Each one had rationalized mitigating circumstances beyond the trivialities of the law, making him special, and innocent.

Both the Jehovah and Angel complexes are Janus-faced. On one hand they fuel our tremendous drive for survival and affirmation, and our ability to be productive and creative. But they can also land us in a lot of trouble.

One bad side effect of our Jehovah complex (I am the center of the universe) is the great difficulty we have in expressing negative emotions, particularly anger. Of course, our upbringing and our social insistence on niceness and good behavior even if it kills us, compound the problem. But deep down we fear our anger because it feels so destructive. Like Jupiter, we are armed with miniature thunderbolts, capable of hurting and alienating the people we love.

A second consequence is that we are all

slightly paranoid. I see two people talking in a corridor. When I pass they fall silent—they must have been discussing *me*. Or three executives lunch together; I wasn't invited—what were they plotting?

Many of our personal problems have been solely generated by our Jehovah complex. One attorney told me he was offended when he went to a public hearing and was moved from his usual place in the front to a seat in the corner. He claimed he had been publicly insulted, brooded over it and took out his feelings on his fellow workers. He made himself so unpleasant that he was fired, and when he came to me he had been out of work for two years, although his abilities and qualifications were impressive.

When we discussed this incident, I suggested the possibility that he had not been pulled back at this meeting, perhaps someone else had been pushed forward. I asked him who had taken his place? He went white as a sheet, then replied: "My God, you are right! Two reporters were given my space. I wasn't pushed back at all—they were given good seats so that they could cover the meeting."

Many years ago, I confess that something similar happened to me. At the time I was operations manager of a big plant. I was working almost around the clock, until one day the president called me in, and said: "Eli, we cannot repay the debt you are creating. We don't want you to work so hard." I didn't take the hint and continued to haunt the place day and night, so the president hired a new manager to take over the second shift. Even though the newcomer was ordered to report to me, I felt his presence was a criticism of my management. I was in a huff, and started such a negative trend that I had to leave the firm.

I almost got carried away by my Jehovah complex during my marriage. It happens that I am a vegetarian, and my wife became one too. Then one day she started bringing home library books on women's lib. At the same time she went out and bought steak and chicken livers for herself. I put two and two together and made five. Of course I didn't really care what my wife ate, but at the time I felt as though she was throwing every chicken liver in my face. Later on we talked about it sensibly, and naturally I cooled down.

Silly as this incident sounds, sudden or unexplained changes can easily invoke domestic paranoia. *She* decides to go out and get a job (don't I make enough money?) or spruces up her appearance (a lover?). *He* starts working late (a mistress?) or going out with the boys (doesn't he love me any more?).

Our Angel complex can have bad side effects, too. We are all familiar with the person who turns the need to be right into a lifelong crusade. At best these people are irritating; at worst they ruin businesses, cause wars or get burned at the stake. And at home, two angels having a scrap can turn into fighting cocks, or snipe at each other for years, just trying to prove that each is right.

Our Angel complex makes it very hard for us to change, even though we are unhappy or unsuccessful. We hug our problems, our depressions, our neuroses, our unhappiness, and build them into a way of life. To get rid of them would mean admitting we were wrong. If we are not careful we end up like Robert Gray, immortalized in an English churchyard by the following epitaph:

> Here lies the body of Robert Gray
> Who died defending his right of way.
> He was dead right, and his case was strong,
> But he was just as dead as if he'd been wrong.

As a corollary, we expect the other person to change or make the first move. A young Florence Nightingale will marry an alcoholic or a Don Juan, convinced that *she* can get *him* to change. Of course she finds she is married to an Angel, unliveable with, perhaps, but right. Even if she succeeds in reforming him, the relationship may crash, since he is no longer the person she married, and both will have acquired different needs and interests. More likely she will fail, and they will wind up in therapy or in the divorce court insisting that everything would be fine if only their mate reformed. Doing as you would be done by is all very well—if the other person does it first.

Coming to grips with your own paranoia becomes much easier if you remember an extremely important principle which is the direct outcome of our instinct to choose what is favorable to us and our self-centered Jehovah complex. The rule is: *People, in the first instance, do not do things for you or against you, but for themselves. It is your fortune, good or bad, to be in the way.*

Obviously this is not true one-hundred percent of the time. You probably have, or will, encounter people who are sick or vicious enought to hurt you gratuitously. There are also enlightened people, like you and me, who will do something *good* for people. But the rule is still true in most situations.

The first question to ask yourself when your paranoia button has been pressed is whether the people or institutions are *really* doing something against you, or simply *for* them-selves? Here are some examples.

A business executive recently rushed in to

me and said in a panic: "Something terrible has happened! I have been reporting to our firm's president. All of a sudden they've announced the president and chief assistant are moving their offices to a new building. The rest of us are to be left behind, and are to report to the general manager, who will be our only link with the president. They have down-graded me!"

This executive was convinced he was on his way out. But I suggested: "Let's assume no one was thinking of you, each person thinks primarily of himself. Is there any valid reason why the president wants to separate his activities from the rest of the group?" It turned out the president specialized in selling, public relations, raising money and impressing people. He wanted premises with carpets half-a-foot high, to snow visiting executives, all part of the old look-rich game. In a little while, my visitor realized this move made good sense. No one had thought of down-grading him; no one had thought of him at all, he had been hit accidentally.

Another businessman told me his firm was being reorganized, but he hadn't received the raise he expected. Thinking no one appreciated him, and his future there was poor, he decided to send out his resume. "Wait a minute," I told him. "You say the firm is reorganizing. Maybe nobody has had the time to tell you about your raise, or even decide if and when you are due for one. Give them a little more time, don't move just yet." A week later he was back, beaming and pulling on a fat cigar. His raise had come through.

A woman told me that she and her husband weren't getting along well. He was moody, depressed and quarrelsome; she was at her wits' end. After attending one of my seminars, she pondered my statement about people in the first instance not doing things for you or against you, but for themselves. She rethought her marital situation, and told me: "I was really beginning to believe my husband was out to get me, that he didn't love me any more. Now I believe he's more bothered by other problems he can't talk about." Feeling more sympathetic, she made a fresh attempt to communicate with him, and he responded. Has anything like this happened to you?

Besides coming to terms with your own paranoia, you should be very careful not to press the panic button in others. Let's re-examine the earlier examples. When my wife and I were quarreling over the chicken livers, she was eventually able to explain that her changed diet had nothing to do with her interest in the women's movement. She was doing both things for herself, which I agreed was the best reason for doing anything, after which neither the liberation nor the livers bothered me in the slightest.

Today many marriages are being drastically overhauled as women, in particular, want fewer children (or none), their own careers, equal rights, shared housework and even new sexual arrangements. Important and necessary as these things may be, they should be discussed as openly and lovingly as possible. Else madam will get Jehovah on his high horse, and she will get it all flung back at her with the force of a threatened male ego. If she can explain she needs to do these things for herself, for his sake, or for the family, *not* against him, he may very well agree with her.

If explanation does not work immediately, be patient. In the new world of women's liberation, for instance, where women have taken meticulous care to explain to men what they are about, and now feel completely justified in all their actions, they are often dismayed to find the man seemingly ignoring, contradicting or being unaware of the new attitudes to which he has agreed. He is merely falling back into the comfort of the habit patterns built up over many years.

In the two cases I mentioned when a client and I both panicked ourselves out of good jobs, we obviously could blame no one but ourselves. But the situation could have been helped if our bosses had taken the time to explain, patiently, until we got the point, exactly what they were doing, and why. In all probability we would not have reacted the way we did.

When *any* changes are in the wind—explain, and keep on explaining. It will become easier when you remember that secrecy is the power of children, not the strength of adults. If you take refuge in "it's none of their business," "they wouldn't understand," or "corporation policy," you may well find the atmosphere at home or work as friendly as a snake pit.

People who wear paranoia on their sleeves need particularly careful handling. One friend told me about a bad experience with his supervisor, a jittery and paranoid lady, who distrusted everyone but him, simply because he told her everything that went on. Then one day a colleague slipped him a note, containing nothing more than a dirty joke. Not wishing to embarrass her, he concealed it. Unfortunately she saw, suspected the worst and never trusted him again.

In coming to terms with your Angel complex, it helps to look back at all those instances when you simply *had* to be right. How did the other people react, and was the payoff worth it? Maybe your target should be to feel good enough about yourself to permit the occasional luxury of being wrong, admitting you don't know, or at least not beating people over the head with your moral rectitude. If you can do it, other people will respond more favorably. You will also be able to justify it to yourself as right, a powerful tool for making *any* changes in your own life or attitudes. Once you have decided to start on a new course, you not only have to complete it, you have to be right. You are still an angel, but off on a new tack, and glowing with the additional virtue of being righter-than-right.

Meanwhile, remember another important human relations principle: *Never tell people they are wrong.* By doing so you deny their validity, and trigger the full force of their (now wounded) Angel complex. So desperately do we need to be right, that any discussion in which you tell people they aren't, nearly always ends in reinforcing their wrongness, not correcting it.

The horror of telling people they are wrong is amusingly illustrated by its opposite. When you pay friends a compliment, in effect telling them they are beautifully right, they will often pretend a temporary deafness. "I beg your pardon! What did you say?" (Meaning, I want to hear that again! Stroke me twice!)

If you are in the odious position of having to correct somebody, here are some other approaches you might try. One is the charming Socratic method; a sweet "yes, but . . . " followed by a gentle questioning, during which the other person has room to do an about-face, let the super-Angel come into play, and admit, not perhaps error, but that doing something else would be even more right. For example, when your secretary types something that doesn't look quite right, tell her it's beautiful, but wouldn't it look nicer or be more legible if she had, say, used wider margins or a different line spacing?

Another good way is to depersonalize your criticism. If it is a child at the receiving end, stress that he or she did a bad thing, not that he or she is actually bad. With an adult, put your complaint in writing—then sit on it overnight (la nuit porte conseil) particularly if the subject is a sensitive one.

Try it! Also try telling people they are wrong directly. You will find that they may not even hear you. If you *do* penetrate their ego barrier on an important issue, they will smite you as surely as the Angel of Death.

PRINCIPLES

We all have a Jehovah complex, making us feel we are the center of the universe.
We are all Angels—everything we do has to be right.

People, in the first instance, do not do things for you or against you, but for themselves. It is your fortune, good or bad, to be in the way.

Never tell people they are wrong directly.

EXERCISES

1. Think of instances where your Jehovah complex has made you paranoid, and you mishandled situations. What did you

do—what happened—and what should you have done? Are you presently in such a situation, and can you correct it?

2. Now do the same exercise thinking of your partner, friends, employers and employees, past and present. If someone close to you is currently in trouble because of Jehovah complex problems, can you discuss it with him or her?

3. Think about your own Angel complex. How do you act on your need to be right —and how does this affect others? Do you lecture, or argue? Are you a know-all, or a bully? Are there any ways you unconsciously put people down? Now discuss your thoughts with your husband or wife or (if you have one, and can talk without losing face) your secretary.

4. Play the old game of They are, You are, I am, writing down 10 or more examples in your notebook to illustrate people's Angel complexes. Examples:

(a) He is as fat as a hog, you are over-
    weight, I am pleasingly plump.
(b) She screeches, you have a high voice, I
    am a soprano.
(c) He is a real nut, you are different, I am
    unique.

4

THE UNREASON
OF REASON

A stockbroker I know recently moved himself
and his accounts to a new brokerage house.
True to the custom of his business, he gave
notice in the morning, cleaned out his desk and
files and was settled in his new office by lunch
time. But the move was painful for him, he had
worked for his old firm for 18 years, so he
broke down and wept. A new colleague re-
marked: "You *are* emotional, aren't you?" A
chill passed through my friend, in case his

momentary lapse (or honesty) might give him a fatal reputation for being unstable. Yet at the same time he was angry at not being permitted to express his true feelings.

The myth that we are a rational society dies hard. We tend to forget an extremely important principle of human relations, namely that *all reaction is instinctively emotional*. The immediate response to anything seen, felt, touched, tasted, smelled, thought or anticipated, is an emotional one. Reason only catches emotion after it is in flight. Oh, it does so very rapidly. On most occasions you can hardly feel the tightness in your jaw before the cool voice of judgment captures your anger, or hardly note the tug of desire before the rational mind yells: "Danger! Danger!"

The purpose of our emotions is to provide (sometimes not too cleverly) the ultimate life affirmation, immortality. This drive is the generator of all our acquisitive instincts, and as important to us as hunger, thirst, sex and the need for sleep and warmth. Our rational, conscious mind is an afterthought, acting as a filter and translator of the original feeling, making it socially acceptable, so that we can continue to act in a way that will permit us to survive by triggering an appropriate response from other people.

For example, you are walking down the street and someone stomps on your toe. Your immediate reaction is to turn and attack the other person. Then they mutter an excuse me, and your rational mind identifies it as an accident. Reason has made the hurt acceptable, and it also allows you, openly or silently, to bawl out the stomper, providing a substitute for murder.

Backing up our emotions and our reason are three other elements: our subconscious, conscience and imagination.

One function of the subconscious is to act as an automatic pilot. We do something six times, like cleaning our teeth, and it becomes a habit, we are hardly aware of continuing to do it.

Conscience serves as a technical auditing center, recording positive and negative events—life perpetuating or life destructive

—and labels them as such for future reference. When we set out to do something, the rational mind, even while translating our thoughts, will send them for evaluation to the conscience. We get an answer: "Proceed, no bad reports," or "Sorry, red lights blinking, you may be in trouble."

A human being, at the instant appreciation level (which is always an emotional one) takes every action as being zero or one, either for me or against me. Recorded as such, every action and reaction is fed into our memory core for future retrieval. There is nothing, once recorded, that is not remembered, or could be remembered, possibly under the influence of stress, drugs, meditation or hypnosis.

Let us go back to our emotions, since these are the key to understanding ourselves, our reactions to other people and theirs to us. Once we understand our emotions and can handle them, we have an enormously powerful tool for avoiding or smoothing out problem situations, and for selecting positive rather than negative messages for our own and other people's memory core.

One characteristic of our emotions is that, like Cupid, they are blind. We want something because we want it, or hate certain people just because we hate them, having the feeling is its own justification.

The ancient Greeks used to account for this by describing a quarrel between Love and Folly, during which Folly poked out Love's eyes. As a punishment, the gods condemned her to lead Love, whom she had blinded, forever by the hand.

I prefer to think that many of our likes and dislikes are imposed on us by our irrational Angel complex. In anger at someone or something, or even in our ignorance, we repeat our dislike over and over again until it becomes a habit, whether the victim is oysters, blacks, foreigners, or a different way of love-making.

Our emotions have no sense of time; they are immediate, they also demand eternity. It only needs one flash, a perfume or a tune, and we are instantly back to an emotional moment in time perhaps many years ago, with our original feelings still fresh.

67

How many people do you know who decided to get married or live together almost the instant they met? I remember asking one young woman friend how she met her husband. She replied: "It was very strange. We met, looked at each other, and ten minutes later he asked me to marry him. We hadn't even spoken until then, but we felt a kind of electricity." Love at first sight is only possible because our emotions have no sense of time. When someone says: "I love you," they frequently add: "I feel as if I have always known you."

In the same way, when you are happy, you think you have been happy forever—sometimes it is the other way around. How often do you say: "You never listen to me," or: "You are always nagging?" Or a guy tells his girlfriend she is a good cook, on the strength of three good meals (maybe only one). Sometimes an office manager says: "We have always done things this way," starting last month.

For this reason, it is vital to your life and happiness that you love what you are doing.

When your work is stimulating, creative and challenging, it involves all your emotional and mental powers. Hours can go by in a single moment. But if you are bored, unhappy, anxious or in danger, time seems to stop, and you are trapped in the endless, eternal minute that drags on forever.

Our emotions also have no sense of weight. You may recall my earlier examples of the woman who killed her husband because he couldn't play good bridge and the Frenchman who liquidated two wives who couldn't cook. Murders are committed almost every day for what looks like no reason. People start arguments in bars, cars and buses, then pull out guns and slaughter each other. Less seriously, don't you get worked up into a murderous rage when another driver tailgates you, cuts ahead on the freeway or bangs into your parked car without leaving a note of apology?

Much of this seemingly odd behavior is caused by the fact that our emotions have a scale of values determined by our Jehovah complex. We could call this a law of inverse distance: my reaction depends on how closely something affects me, and the farther away something happens, the less I care. Hence *my* cut finger is more important than *your* broken leg. *We* are more important than the plane crash which killed 50 people outside Paris. Americans are more important than Asians, Africans or Indians, even if these happen to be starving.

Another characteristic of our emotions is that, because they are blind, they will accept substitutions. If necessary, they will even accept a dream instead of the real thing. When I see a pretty woman in the street, my immediate desire is to make love to her. By the time my emotion has expressed itself, reason has advised me to watch out, so I walk by and grin or give her an admiring look or if I feel brave, maybe pay her a compliment.

Real life, perhaps unfortunately, is stuffed with such substitutions. Politicians promise tax reform, parents promise a trip to the circus —emotionally, it is as good as done. The radical left and right shower each other with political rhetoric, and the long hairs or capitalist pigs are as good as dead. A furious mob gathers outside an embassy and howls: "Down with the foreigners!" then trails home tired but happy that the foreigners have, in a sense, fallen.

This power of substitution can easily become a way of life. A busy husband showers his wife and kids with presents because he cannot or will not take time to be with them. A lonely woman, whose husband does not love her, or whose children have left home, lavishes her affection on the cat. The characters in *The Iceman Cometh* prefer their drunken dreams to the reality of trying to make them come true. What kind of emotional substitutions do *you* have in your life—and do they really substitute, or have they become absurd?

A comptroller I knew, who used to work endless hours, would complain that when he *did* come home his wife was very unfriendly. She would shoo the children out of the way, hide behind the evening paper and finally fix him a dinner he did not like. His wife told me she was fed up with seeing the whole household revolve around long-suffering daddy. In the end he realized that although his original purpose had been to work hard and make his family happy, he ended up making them suffer. All his hard work only caused them unhappiness while the only pleasure he got was playing the martyr.

The harder we look at everyday situations, the clearer we can see the emotional component behind them. This is true even in the "rational" business world. What could be more emotional than the rise and fall of the Dow Jones Average, or marketing men's projection of demand on the basis of consumer confidence?

Many business people, who pride themselves on being hard-headed, really make their decisions on the basis of emotion. You submit a memo to your department head, recommending changes which he isn't going to like because they threaten his Jehovah complex. He says: "Very interesting. Give me time to think about it." One week later your memo is still on

the bottom of his in-tray, or he will call you in
to give you the "rational" reasons why he
cannot implement your suggestions.

Nearly all hiring decisions are ultimately
made for emotional reasons, simply because
there is no objective, scientific way to evaluate
the candidates. In the end you will hire people
because you like them, and you will get the job
because your face seems to fit.

Decisions involving race, age or sex, are also
heavily charged with emotion, usually prejudice. Teenagers say :"Never trust anybody
over 30. They are square, stick-in-the-mud
and have forgotten what it feels like to be
young." Employers sneer at people over 55
(even over 40). They are "too inflexible, they
find it hard to learn, or their memory is poor."
Top management still tends to overlook wom-
en. If they are young, they will take time off
to have children. If they have a young family,
they will be questioned minutely about their
child care arrangements. If they are much over
40 they are "menopausal" and all of them are

"too emotional." In every case the original feeling will be rationalized, and if necessary supported by facts, statistics or experience.

Attitudes to money are charged with emotion. When gaining, it seems life affirmative; when it's lost, the opposite. One woman told me her husband would give handfuls of money away to good causes, but if anyone defaulted on a loan, this threatened Angel would take him to court. She added: "He'll give me an expensive piece of jewelry for my birthday, but bawl me out if I get a parking ticket."

From time to time our emotions bubble out into the open. So long as they are pleasant, all is well. But if we express anger, grief or rejection, we may be in trouble.

When we say someone lost his temper, what do we mean? Simply that the explosion was so violent that the rational mind let slip its grasp. The event expressed itself emotionally by a punch in the jaw, a knife in the back, a scream or tears. And we all have our breaking point—perhaps caused by fatigue, threats, hunger or chemicals—when our mind will no

74

longer verify the reasonableness of our
feelings, or make a palatable solution for the
outside world. When did this last happen to
you?

Yet it is a very important principle of human
relations that *most people will be directly emotional
whenever they can get away with it,* that is when
they feel secure enough to act out their
feelings.

The commonest place where this happens is,
of course, at home. Jehovah comes home after
·a hard day at the office, and takes it out on his
wife. The children take it out on the parent
closest to them, on each other or on the cat.
The woman takes it out on anyone who will
take it, often the whole family.

People readily let down their hair when they
are among equals. They will also act emotionally towards subordinates, like maids, cab
drivers, ticket clerks and waiters. They will
do the same if they think no one is listening, like former President Nixon during
some of the Watergate tapes.

Many adults will be emotional with some-

one they regard as a parent figure. One
highly paid, successful business executive
would always act like a whiny five-year old
whenever he came to see me. Presumably this
was behavior which used to work with
mommy and daddy, and which he never grew
out of.

At the other end of the stick, bosses can
afford to behave emotionally towards their
subordinates, resulting in the unpredictability
which motivated the Biblical saying: "The
heart of the king is unknown."

This behavior will change sharply if there is
a shift in the balance of power. Anyone who is
being beaten emotionally by his boss is perfectly safe. But if the boss decides to fire you, in
his mind you are no longer an employee, and
thus he cannot get away with being emotional.
You need never fear the boss who whips; fear
one who treats you with cold, measured cour-
tesy, for here is the shadow of the guillotine.

Any time we let our negative emotions run
riot, we end up behaving like a four or five year

old child. We hit, shout, weep or sulk. We blame someone else, or failing this, the time-honored ghostly scapegoat: them. They don't know what they are doing. That's the production department's fault. It broke down. Or, it's society's fault. Instead of facing real problems and looking for a rational solution, we scramble to blame someone else, and avoid our own responsibilities.

Anger becomes easier to handle if we remember the earlier principle that people do not, in the first instance, do things either *for* or *against* us, but for themselves, and it is our good or bad fortune to be in the way. We may find we have been wounded accidentally; what really hurts is our own paranoia.

We should try to use the power of substitution to get rid of our rage in some neutral way—punch a ball, jog, swim, pound the piano, scrub the floor or whatever—until our adrenalin level subsides. In short, we should grow up enough to take out our hostility on the cup, rather than the tit. Attacking other people hurts; it also offends their Angel complex, in-validates their sense of themselves, and pro-vokes them to repay in kind.

Obviously you cannot start punching, jog-ging or scrubbing in the middle of a business meeting. But you *can* finger worry beads, doo-dle or (if you must) chew gum. Then, if anger still threatens your control, you can open-end the discussion with a polite excuse, e.g. you need more time to think about what has been said—before you blow up. If you are provoked by your boss or a client, you will have to join what you can't fight. You will quickly be able to rationalize your anger against someone more powerful than you.

Later, try to talk calmly about the reason for your anger, making it clear you are angry at something the other person did, not at *him or her*, and trying to find out the other side of the story; how much is fact, how much wounded ego. Sometimes merely to understand is to forgive. Other times, you may have to work hard to erase a negative in the other person's memory core.

78

One businessman told me how he handled a situation where he was dealing with people who thought he had swindled them. "It was horrible," he said. "We had spent $300,000 of their money; we couldn't account for it, and had no excuse for the errors we had made. We didn't know how to give an answer without making them still angrier. After days of considering the problem we decided to tell the truth—how we had slipped and stumbled and made mistakes. We talked with them for an hour, drawing a chart. They completely changed their attitude, understanding we hadn't deliberately acted against them. In the end we all agreed it was a sad situation—but due to human error, not malice."

A woman told me how she had worked out an angry scene with her husband. They had just moved into a new house, were unpacking their furniture and she was lining shelves in the kitchen closets with fresh paper. Her husband followed her around complaining she wasn't putting the paper on straight. Fatigued with the work of moving, she first lost control and told him where he could go. When she felt calmer, she asked what was *really* bothering him. Sheepishly he explained that he felt unhappy at the move because he felt the new house was not the bargain he had originally thought and would need a lot of work to fix up. They then had an adult discussion about the work which needed to be done and the ugly scene evaporated.

Many other difficult situations are caused not just because we behave like raging five-year-olds, but because something has triggered our Jehovah or Angel complex. We are expressing paranoia or an urgent need to justify ourselves. Committee meetings get out of hand as people push or defend themselves, their programs or their sections. A government department threatened with elimination or reorganization virtually stops dead as its members man the defenses, or simply scramble to save their necks. Executives who feel insecure will squabble over such toys as the furnishings of their offices, the quality of the graphics and the size, color and pile of the carpets.

Any of these feelings can easily get us into a pay and pay back situation which turns into a vendetta. Both sides are Jehovah, and take things personally, and as Angels, must prove themselves right. Each mental computer has registered a series of negatives, so we are bound to repay—and this time it is an eye for an eye.

Imagine you are the president of the corporation which has just moved its executive suite, leaving me behind to stew at the supposed affront. Meeting you, I look sour and uncommunicative. Your memory core is blank with no debts to repay. But now as you sense my nasty attitude, you are going to reciprocate. We have started a bad sequence. I twist your little finger, you pull off two of mine. I break your arm, you stomp on my leg. I stab your back, you gouge out my heart. If we don't stop, this pay and pay back will lead to death, meaning in this case that I will get fired.

Such a vendetta can put any marriage on the rocks, though usually a couple will feud until the situation approaches the point of no return, and in the face of disaster, both pull back. If enough blood has been drawn, the weapons can be put away. If not, the troubles go back into the marital gunnysack, to be pulled out another time.

Other individuals or groups may have fewer scruples. We are all familiar with families or neighbors who never speak to each other— their feuds can remain stalemated for generations. Or a momentum can be achieved that results in endless war or death—like the Arabs and the Israelis or the Irish Catholics and Protestants.

When the vendetta goes on at an unconscious level, the result is cold war. Families indulge in passive-aggressive behavior to try to get what they want, working out their anger or simply paying back in a manner nicely calculated to drive everyone up the wall.

Many of us carry on this kind of war against our parents, particularly the parent we loved

least, or may have even hated, but whose bad
qualities we have somehow managed to inter-
nalize. We blame them, overtly or not, for
spoiling or warping our lives, carrying a sullen
or angry grudge long after they are dead and
buried.

In business, this type of pay and pay back
comes out in what I call leavers' syndrome.
You have decided to leave a company, possibly
under a cloud, and you justify your decision by
starting to criticize the firm. Sometimes you
can't wait to join a rival outfit and do your best
to ruin, or take over, your former employer. Of
course, if the boss is firing *you*, he will not have
a good word to say about you either. In the
words of the French proverb, anyone who
wishes to kill his dog will first accuse it of
rabies.

So when you come to me to give your notice,
I would be the biggest fool if I allowed you to
so much as return to your office. I would say:
"Mr. or Ms. So-and-so, my Cadillac and
chauffeur are outside and I really think you
should have a meal at the Blue Fox. And why

don't you take the family on a vacation? Here's your check, and goodbye." You will walk out congratulating yourself on your sheer guts in daring to give the old monster two months' notice. I will think, good riddance.

Ironically, even a positive pay and pay back trend can get out of hand. In my own case, when I worked night and day to make myself indispensable, my boss frankly admitted I was creating an obligation he could not repay. Other times, in business and politics, favor for favor goes beyond Christmas gifts, special allowances or moderate political contributions, and becomes overt bribery or blackmail.

This can also happen in our personal lives. Some parents "work their fingers to the bone" for each other or their offspring, making such a to-do about their sacrifice that they create the kind of anger and resentment so vividly expressed in *Portnoy's Complaint.* At a less serious level, haven't we all felt obliged to entertain people we didn't like simply because they invited us first?

Behind some of these problems is a failure

of ethics; it is not right or proper to create an obligation which the other person cannot easily repay. There are also a number of techniques to stop a vendetta which I will discuss in Chapter 7. But if you really understand the principle of reciprocity, you can use it in a triumphantly effective way to reverse almost any kind of bad situation. The tools are there for the asking—if you really wish to use them. Everyone in the end has to choose between becoming a radiating force to which others will be drawn, a mirror passively reflecting the world for better or worse, or carrying a knife.

PRINCIPLES

All reaction is instinctively emotional.

Our emotions are blind: they have no sense of time or weight and they will accept substitutions.

Most people will be directly emotional whenever they can get away with it.

All debts and hurts are repaid.

EXERCISES

1. Evaluate your use of your rational mind to overcome a recent emotional reaction.

2. Think of a recent business decision you made. What was the emotional reason for it and how did you justify it to yourself and the other people involved?

3. Now do the same for your boss. What do you think was the underlying emotion and how did he or she rationalize the decision?

4. When was the last time you lost your temper? Why? With whom? What did you do about it? How *should* you have handled the situation?

5. Are you accepting many emotional substitutions, e.g. for love, success or a sense of significance? Do these satisfy you? If not, what can you do about it?

6. Do you give your family gifts—or excuses—for not spending more time with

them? How do they feel about this? What can all of you do to change?

7. What does money *really* mean to you?

8. Are you now engaged in a vendetta with anyone, living or dead? What do you do to pay and pay back? How do you rationalize this? How can the feud be stopped?

5

COMMUNICATING TO PERSUADE

Many of our communications difficulties arise because we attack problems like James Thurber's dog Jeannie, who tried to get out of a garage by digging through the concrete floor with one paw. We constantly think other people will be persuaded by our intelligent presentation of the facts or the force of our convictions—when in reality these glance off them like raindrops off a car roof. We have totally ignored the need to prepare the ground for the emotional climate which will make people listen to us, trust us and be persuaded by our message.

The most important principle to remember is that *each person has a priority list. You are always at the top of your own list—and near the bottom of everyone else's, unless they happen to love you. Then you might be number 2.* This is the direct outcome of the earlier law of inverse distance; my interests are always going to be more urgent than yours. My hangnail is more important than a famine in China.

Our basic priority lists have long been known to marketing, advertising and sales people, who make barely disguised appeals to our universal needs for sex, love, food security and so on. If these appeals are motivated by commercial gain, we often see through (and resist) them rather rapidly. But everybody also has a second priority list: the one that individualizes us, though it may only be these drives reappearing in carnival dress.

To communicate effectively, we must penetrate the other person's priority list, and rise to the top, at least for the time needed for communication. We can nearly always do this by identifying consciously and sincerely with the other person's interests.

At home, a woman who is in hysterics because the washing machine overflowed, and jumps on her husband to fix it the moment he comes in, won't get very far if he has a load of business worries on his chest. On the other hand, he can't expect *her* to show a burning interest in his row with the boss while there is unfinished laundry and a swamp all over the kitchen floor.

Somehow *we must train ourselves emotionally to wear someone else's moccasins*. Suppose your salary is reduced by $1000 or you don't get the raise you want. Two days later your boss comments on how pleased he is with your work. He expects you to be happy—but had he worn your moccasins he might have offered sympathy or allowed you to express your feelings rather than toss you a word of lukewarm praise.

Conversely, one friend, the chief engineer for a manufacturing firm, wrote a superb master plan for the coming year's work. He delivered it to the company president, who was not an engineer, but had a Ph.D. in English. He got it back with every spelling mistake and grammatical error outlined in red. My friend shook with anger. "So what, if there is a split infinitive or I can't spell procrastination. Look at all those red smears! *He's* giving me English lessons when I have given him a plan to boost company profits! I'm through, I'm going to resign!"

I replied: "You've just been paid a compliment. The only thing your president didn't like was your English. He undoubtedly approves of your plan, but he wanted your report properly dressed. Wouldn't you feel the same if language was as important to you as it is to him?"

A good way to identify with other people is to line up wavebands of common interest along which to communicate. If you are a dentist, my toothache band lines up with you. If you are a party-goer and a bridge player, my bridge and party-going bands line up with you. Human interest bands work for anyone we don't know well —your secretary's unhappy love affair, a neighbor's ulcer, a supermarket checker's tired feet.

Establishing common interests can be a slow process, especially in the beginning. However it helps to remember the principle of a little but often. It's interesting that if we see someone for 50 hours continuously, we will know something of that person, perhaps a good deal, but still feel we don't know him or her well. But if we meet an hour a week for 50 weeks, we will feel we *really* know the other person. It is the repetition which is so valuable—a fact well known in advertising and programmed learning. *Repeated contacts, however brief, are better than a single contact in establishing communication.*

Behind the rule that we must identify with other people's interests is the earlier principle of reciprocity. People *must* repay all debts in kind; if you take a friendly human interest in them, they are likely to do the same for you. Also you tickle their Jehovah and Angel complexes by allowing them to sound off about something they care about deeply, and at which they believe they are expert.

People will also respond favorably if your purpose is truly ethical and they feel you have their true interests at heart. We will accept nearly anything from a person in whom we have faith. If we trust our doctor or dentist, we cooperate with them when they prescribe certain drugs, remove a tooth or recommend surgery. If we trust our stockbrokers we will buy and sell at their recommendations. The ideal climate of faith is created by parents, particularly mothers, with their children. So completely do small children believe their parents are acting in their best interests that they allow them to make the major decisions of their lives without questions. They may grumble, but still believe mommy and daddy are gods, at least until adolescence sets in.

Another important principle of communicating to persuade is that of *giving first*. Do as you would be done by has to start with *you*. The Bible states it beautifully: "Cast thy bread upon the waters and it will return after many days." Tragically many lives and opportunities are wasted because we don't want to give first, but either hang back or want to trade.

Some people spend their whole lives without love, waiting for the Right Person to come along. There could have been many right ones if we could have made the first move. We can also get into horrible pay and pay back situations because we refuse to act first to make amends.

Giving first, and identifying with someone else's interests, are very powerful tools for getting what you want. Some understand this almost instinctively. Listen to them on the telephone. They have learned to talk with someone for 20 minutes about the other person's concerns. Only at the very end of the conversation will they slip in the reason for the call. This is the patience that wins, the kindness that wins.

It is easy to use the same tactic to influence a committee. Go in with an ethical purpose, don't deviate from it, but allow others to unblock their minds or air their objections by first talking out their points. Having made their impression, they can gracefully allow you to do what you planned from the beginning. You will not have convinced them—they will have convinced themselves.

Identifying with other people's interests is doubly effective when you learn to *speak their language.* I have found that there are in the main three different types of people, each speaking a different language in terms of mental and emotional reactions.

There is the person who is mainly logical, who has educated himself to pass most emotions through his reason and only use those he finds acceptable. Another type has learned to pass many things directly through the emotions, and make decisions without running them through the rational mind. Then there is the third type who varies, sometimes logical, other times emotional. Remember though, everyone is made up of both logical and emotional parts.

It does not take long to discover whether someone is intensely logical or primarily emotional. Logical people will ask you what you *think* rather than what you *feel* about something. They will also back up their statements with phrases like: it is a matter of observation, it can be statistically proved, it is public knowledge, according to the formula, or *The New York Times* says. The emotional person will say: I have a feeling, I believe, in my opinion, and will usually skip references to other authorities, except, occasionally, "they."

The emotional person will be deaf to logic, and the other way around. So if people talk statistics, drown them in numbers. If they talk in terms of feelings, talk feelings, moods, form, color and texture. If they are in between, try both approaches. If (like many nonverbal types) they find it hard to talk at all, reach them with graphs, schematics and diagrams.

If someone is concerned about woman's liberation, you must talk women's lib. You don't have to go to extreme lengths of language distortion, like saying peoplekind for mankind, but you could compromise on humanity. Play safe by saying chairperson and changing sexist nouns and pronouns into more neutral ones.

One young woman who came to see me was an artist. All I had been told was that she was unhappy and my total conversation with her was: "I understand that you're in the business world and you're unhappy and you want to return to a world of color and form." And she said: "Yes." I replied: "We will help you get to that world. I would like to ask you a favor. When our work is complete, will you have dinner with me, because I feel I could learn much from your sensitivity?" She accepted. Then as she left, she took my hand and said: "This was the most wonderful conversation I have had in years." I had really said very little, but internally I was feeling an empathy with her pain and communicating this to someone to whom words would mean little anyway.

Underlying the spoken or written word is the fascinating world of nonverbal communication. Some of our signals are paraverbal—we grunt, groan, mutter and sniff. Others are kinetic—body language. We shrug, stare, cross

our legs, wink or raise an eyebrow to communicate clearly what we feel. There is also the
inaudible band, a direct appeal of emotion to
emotion. It can occur across miles and time in
the form of telepathy or ESP. We use it to signal
people close to us. Often communication with
a loved one needs a minimum of words. All
these ways employ the lightning time sense of
our emotions; the message is conveyed with a
speed that mere words cannot accomplish.

One young man who was completely blind
used to come in and sit in front of me and say:
"Eli, you're edgy today!" I hadn't spoken a
word. Not only that but when I was working
with him, feelings would be sensed across the
table to a phenomenal degree, and I quickly
forgot I was talking to a blind person. Later on,
I introduced him to the young woman artist.
She would read aloud to him in the library for
hours on end, and afterwards he told me: "She
was fantastic! Without my mentioning a word,
she would repeat the important passages,
every one of which I wanted repeated." Some
inaudible input was guiding her to do it.

We should also be careful to study the body language of members of our family and the people we meet. Are you always aware of the relaxed expression and gestures which signal *yes*, or at least an openness to what you have to say? Do you know the subtle signs meaning *come on*, the crossed arms and legs, withdrawn chin, closed or averted eyes and hunched shoulders which mean *no*, or *I am not interested . . . I disagree . . . leave me alone*? In an interview or business meeting can you spot the body language that conveys power and status, and who in the meeting will unconsciously copy the leader's gestures, signaling agreement and solidarity with the boss?

Behind these different verbal and nonverbal languages we will find certain basic ways in which people try to get what they want, namely security. Why security? One story of life is that we are each thrown out of our mother's womb, suffering at birth an ugly form of rejection. Waving our tiny arms and legs at an unfriendly world, we pant for breath and seek a way to return to the security we left behind. We choose one of six main highways.

100

One road is love. "If they love me, I'll get what I want." Baby finds this doesn't always work—though in later life it will be tried again on a lover. So baby screams madly, taking the second road, force. A third is to submit to conquer. A fourth is to be an opportunist, "bending with the willow, not with the oak." A fifth road is habit, that is power through automatic response; a sixth, wealth. But all end at the same destination—security.

Most people do not choose one path and walk it forever. They may try all roads at different times. It is easy to identify which road a particular person is traveling. Lonely prophets preach love so crowds will encircle them to cure their loneliness. Philosophers withdraw into caves, constructing a cobweb of reason to force all people to them. Artists paint to reveal their private fantasies to a gallery of eyes, present and unborn.

All of us ransack our private arsenal for weapons we hope will bring an instant return. We bully or blackmail, manipulate, grovel, flatter, chatter or just smile a lot. But there are still only six roads, and three kinds of passengers traveling them. When you can identify the road and the type of person embarked upon it, both of you can talk the same language.

How does this relate to communication? You come to me with force and threats and I see that force and threats work on you, so I will use them. You come with gifts and love and I know these work with you. "As you are to me, so am I to you." As you communicate with me, so I communicate with you.

PRINCIPLES

Each person has a priority list. You are always at the top of your own list—and near the bottom of everyone else's unless they happen to love you. Then you might be number 2.

Train yourself emotionally to wear someone else's moccasins.

Communicate with people by identifying common interests.

Repeated contacts, however brief, are better than a single contact, however long, in establishing communication.

102

Give first.

Learn to speak another person's language.

People seek security by traveling six roads—love, force, submission, flexibility, habit and wealth.

EXERCISES

1. What methods do you use to get what you want? Your partner? The children? Your boss?

2. How do you communicate without words? How well does your partner receive and understand your messages?

3. Next time your family is quarreling, try this experiment: don't speak, just act out your feelings (everyone) and see what happens.

4. Listen to the way your partner, children and boss speak. Are they mainly logical, emotional or a mixture. What verbal clues do they give?

5. Think of the last time you tried to persuade someone to take a new point of view. How

103

did you do this, and with what result? How would you do it differently now?

6. Observe a person you do not know well, and write a description of the ways he or she communicates without words. What would his or her priority list look like?

7. Listen to some of your favorite music daily for 10 minutes. What are some of the feelings, thoughts and images the composer or singer is trying to convey?

8. Think of an incident when your choice of words or use of body language led to a misunderstanding. What happened, how and why?

6

TWO CONTRASTS IN COMMUNICATION

One day some visitors to my office brought in
their two nursery-school aged children, a boy
and a girl. Hoping to bribe them to be seen and
not heard, my secretary offered each a big
piece of chocolate and ate a third herself. A few
moments later, the little boy bounced up and
demanded another chocolate. His sister was
more subtle. She timidly approached the desk,
smiled and asked: "Have you finished your
chocolate? Are you going to have another?"

Differences in attitude and communication style start early in life, and they are so profound that most adults are never quite able to put their finger on precisely why they exist and how they work. Yet understanding them allows us to predict reactions more accurately and deal more effectively with others. It also enables us to temper our own reactions, sidestepping many verbal battles.

Some people fight to desperation, sometimes throwing away a war to win a single battle. Others will greet the invader with flowers and cheers, on the theory that if you can't beat'em, join 'em. Historically, whole races have on occasions chosen one or the other reaction: they have fought and been exterminated, or given in, and eventually conquered their conquerors.

Psychologists like to explain the difference sexually by saying that the male feels compelled to defend an idea or a possession, while the female needs to ensure the safety of the brood. Even more likely is the harsh reality of

106

power—physical, social, political and economic—which has rarely been on the woman's side, and forces her from childhood to become an expert survivor and manipulator.

When the locus of power changes, the sexes may pull a switch. A man cannot be too dominating with his boss or an important client, but is forced, often reluctantly, into a subservient position. A woman dealing with small children will often order them around like a marine commander.

Advancing age can also bring changes in the traditional approach. Young and middle-aged men are often trained by their role as family breadwinner to be dominating and aggressive, while women may become more compliant and passive to contrast with the dominant role they take with children. But in later life many men gratefully sink into sweetness and puttering, training to become affable old grandpas, while their women plunge into new careers.

These are general principles which explain

an important difference between two types of people: *one dominates to conquer, while the other submits to conquer.*

The direct versus the indirect approach also carries over into communication styles. For one a question is a question and a statement is a statement. But for the other, it is not so simple. The indirect person *does not make statements, he asks questions, and he does not ask questions, he makes statements.*

These people make a statement when they want to ask a question on an important issue because a statement is a challenge. Challenged, the other person's first impulse is to say: "That isn't true, and here's why." The indirect person quickly agrees because the whole procedure was designed to test the water, to focus attention on the matter and make the other person think it through. The object of this method may be furious if he sees through it, but will now make up his mind.

You can ask a question, transferring the burden of decision to the other person, gently hinting at the outcome, while allowing him to retain his feeling of dominance. You also avoid rejection if the answer is no. It is a superb way for getting around a Jehovah complex!

One businessman told me how it worked in his family. "We are on a tight budget," he explained. "We save money and everything is under control" (meaning, of course, *his*). "But last week my wife said: 'The children need Levis and shirts.' A little later she added: 'The Emporium and Macy's are having sales on Levis and shirts.' Still later she asked: "What do you think we should do about the sales at the Emporium and Macy's?'"

Subliminally, this man's logic had been coaxed into play. He woke up and said: "The obvious thing to do is to buy some." His wife asked: "We're not going to play golf this afternoon?" He replied: "We'd better take the kids to the sale." She conceded: "Fine, if that's what you want to do." Suddenly he realized what had happened: "I found we had spent $60 completely outside the budget and *I* was the one who made the decision."

Trouble between the two types of people

usually arises when they cannot decide whether a question is really a question or a statement really a statement. Sometimes one will fight a statement for hours, thinking it is an invitation to debate. If you reply to a question like: "Must we have your mother over for Sunday dinner?" by snapping: "You don't get on with my mother, do you?" the fat is in the fire.

A different type of situation can result when two people are under stress, and change their usual ways of reacting. Conflict also erupts on a broader front when both sides behave with excessive directness. No one can do this all the time and assuming that styles are fixed is a mistake. In reality everyone needs to be able to switch in response to mood and situation.

Never ignore the principle of reciprocity. If you come on like a lion, you will be met with a roar. If you start name-calling, you will be insulted back and if you are rawly sensitive to discrimination, real or imagined, you will provoke more of the same. Most people under attack will also try the ancient Syrian remedy

—bring out a lyre, hum a lullaby, and gently back away into the bushes. This is a marvelous way of dealing with someone's Jehovah complex!

In the field of business relations, both the direct and indirect approaches are valuable tools for communication—provided you know when to use them. The direct method is best used as a challenge, to get your boss to make up his mind on an important issue.

Perhaps you need confirmation of your plan or attitude? Shock your boss into opposition by making a statement, and find out his or her real opinion. If your boss agrees with you, you can be sure you are on firm ground. If not, you can do a graceful about-turn and say you are glad to have been straightened out.

One good way of communicating with your boss, again using the direct method, is in writing. List your priorities with regard to work, and discuss them. You have probably studied your boss enough to know which items top his or her priority list. Every time you can interpret *your* plans as relating to those priorities

111

you will find an attentive, sensitive and concerned ear. But if your two lists do not match, you will hear soon enough. Either way, your list serves as a challenge. And your net gain is closer identification with your boss's overall goals and an increase in your value and usefulness through the intelligent feedback you have provided.

This direct approach is also essential with junior employees and, usually, young children. They expect a god, a firm hand of authority, a strong personality leading the way. They expect you to make statements when you are making statements, ask questions when you are asking questions and not to confuse them with too much choice. They (and everyone else, for that matter) also like you to present your ideas in a positive way. If you cannot, then keep quiet.

At the same time you must not forget that everyone still has Jehovah and Angel complexes, including the very small. While you are setting goals and providing the ground rules, you will get more cooperation if these are stated in terms of the other person's interests.

You will also get people to accept criticism if you do not directly tell them they are wrong, but use a modified Socratic questioning until they can spot the error themselves.

Supposing you are *not* the boss? Then the harsh fact about the person above you (however much you do or do not like and respect him) is that he is Batman, while you are only Robin, and in the last resort has the power to chop off your head. In most instances, the direct approach is too dangerous. But study your boss carefully. Often secretaries handle bosses easily. Their secret is simply to ask questions and avoid rejection by giving the boss the privilege of making decisions.

You may find that secretarial questions are well-concealed statements about business decisions. When *my* secretary says: "Would you be thinking about having lunch with Mr. Smith?" I may or may not realize that I am being quietly TOLD to do so. I will probably ask her to reserve the table and think it was my own idea. If she asks me when I would like Mr. Doe to use the closed-circuit TV to test his interviewing skills, I will grandly set a time, still assuming I made the big decision myself.

The way to handle people upwards is with an indirect approach on all important occasions, particularly when you are proposing something controversial. Asking questions, even making a joke about it, will leave you a back door through which to retreat without losing face should the answer happen to be no. If your boss likes the idea, even co-opts it, you will have won a couple of gold stars, which, under the principle of reciprocity, will be repaid later.

Eventually you may find yourself in a situation where neither the direct nor the indirect approach seem to be satisfactory. Either you are being severely threatened, or you are having to threaten somebody else.

Suppose your boss orders you to do something unfair or unethical—or get fired. Under the rule *of joining what you cannot fight* you may knuckle under, but your Angel will certainly be angry and resentful. But suppose you come to work late seven days in a row and your boss tells you to arrive at nine like everyone else or here's the front door. You will be angry momentarily, but your conscience and your *super Angel* will tell you he is right and that you have been performing in contradiction to your better self.

A threat made in conformity with accepted social ethics may not be forgotten, but will not leave residual bad feeling. However, threats and fears should be used as seldom as possible, and only if you are positive they are life-affirming or (as the law is) codified in cold written statements beyond emotionalism. If you have to threaten somebody, be ethical, and then impersonalize it in writing. Otherwise, you will one day be repaid. As the Arabs say: "When the lion falls, the knives multiply," and, if you are not already dead or skewered, you will be in the middle of an ugly vendetta which could have been avoided.

PRINCIPLES

People use two methods: some dominate to conquer, others submit to conquer.

Some do not make statements, they ask questions, and do not ask questions, they make statements.

On all important occasions, use an indirect approach with people more powerful than you, and a direct approach with people less powerful.

You will usually have to join what you cannot fight.

If you must threaten somebody, be ethical, and depersonalize your threat in writing.

EXERCISES

1. When was the last time that you:
   (a) told someone he was wrong?
   (b) tried to persuade someone of something important?
   How did you do this and how successful were you? How would you do it now?

2. How would you try to:
   (a) criticize
   (b) persuade

116

a dominating or short-tempered boss, mate or relative?
Ask two other people how they would do this, and compare notes.

3. Analyze the way you and your partner try to persuade or influence or criticize each other.

4. Analyze the way you relate and give directions to your employees. Could this be improved?

7

TURNING THE RIGHT SIDE UP—OR, HOW TO DEAL WITH THE MAFIA

"I am tired and sick of war. Its glory is all moonshine. It is only for those who have neither fired a shot nor heard the shrieks and groans of the wounded to cry aloud for blood, more vengeance, more desolation. War is Hell."

Sooner or later war catches up with the most Angelic of us, not just the literal kind, which

William Sherman was complaining about, but a vendetta or stalemate in our personal lives. These can also be hell, but there are many human-relations tools you can use to stop the fight and start a new, positive trend.

Like every good general you should take stock of your position, remembering the important points raised earlier in this book. Is it possible you could have exaggerated or even imagined the trouble? There are many times when we all get carried away by our Jehovah or Angel complex. We forget that people in the first instance do not do things for us or against us, but only for themselves, and that we can get hurt accidentally. We also forget that we are lower down on other people's priority lists than we would like, even those of our nearest and dearest.

Is it also possible that you have complicated situations by making up other people's minds for them? How often have we all made the mistake of anticipating someone else's feelings ("he wouldn't like this"), or abilities ("she couldn't do that") and opinions ("he would never give anyone my age a job"). The truth is, *we can never make up other people's minds for them.*

You may remember the story about the man who was driving along a lonely country road at night, got a flat tire, but had no jack in the car and could not put on the spare. Seeing a lighted farmhouse nearby, he decided to try and borrow one. But as he started walking, the place went dark. "Now the farmer has gone to bed," he thought. "He'll probably be annoyed I got him up. And he'll probably want some money for his jack. All right, I'll say, it isn't very neighborly, but here's a quarter. And he'll say: 'Do you think you can get me out of bed in the middle of the night and offer me a quarter? Give me a dollar, or get a jack somewhere else!' All right, a dollar but not a cent more. A poor guy has an accident and all he needs is a jack! You probably won't let me have one no matter how much I pay you!"

By the time he had reached the farmhouse, the man had worked himself into a real rage and thumped angrily on the door. The farmer stuck his head out of the window and hollered:

"Who's there, and what do you want?" The
fellow stopped pounding and yelled back:
"You and your damn jack! I don't want your
jack anyhow!" Next time *you* catch yourself
making up someone else's mind for him, ask
yourself: "Want to borrow a jack?"

Let us now assume that you *are* in trouble,
and that this is real not imagined. It may seem
depressingly insurmountable, until you think
how many *positive* facts about human nature
are on your side. First, *it is more natural for people
to seek friends than enemies,* no matter now sour or
feisty they appear. Of course, you will have to
make the first move, but if you *can* give first
you may be astonished at the good response. If
you cannot, is it because you are too physically
or emotionally low to make the effort, are you
harboring too much unresolved anger or are
you secretly rather enjoying the fight?

A second point to remember is the emotional way everyone responds to situations.
The more personally they are affected, the
more sharply they will react. Emotions can be
dynamite, but they will accept substitutions, a

fact which can help you stop an ugly pay-back. Since emotions have no ordinary sense of time or weight, you can also short-circuit a lot of grief by starting a positive trend which will erase bad feelings in the twinkling of an eye. True, people never forget, but they can forgive—instantly. Suddenly the sky is clear, and seems to have been clear forever. In the marvelously evocative lines from The Song of Solomon:

> For, lo, the winter is past, the rain is over and
> gone.
> The flowers appear on the earth, the time of
> singing has come,
> and the voice of the turtle dove is heard in our
> land.

One way to clear the air is to explain what happened; another, to make reparation. If you borrow my jacket on a snowy day and manage to lose my wallet containing $100, I will be satisfied if you explain it was an accident and give me back $100 out of your own pocket. (I would feel even warmer towards you if you also present me with a new wallet.)

123

If your problem cannot be so easily solved, you will have to *plant a rose to smother the weeds of a bad situation.* In other words, you create a diversion by doing something nice for the person you have been fighting, to which he or she must respond under the law of reciprocity. The favor must be chosen with considerable skill and imagination. You need to be sensitive enough to the other person's wants and feelings to do something that will really be appreciated, without saddling the person with the embarrassment of a debt which looks suspiciously like a bribe or that is difficult to repay.

Here are some simple examples of successful "roses." The children are quarreling at dinner and the mealtime is getting out of hand so you quickly but firmly change the subject to something of great interest to them. Your toddler is playing with sharp scissors and screams when you remove them, but is delighted when you get out the crayons and let him start drawing. A teenage girl who has been bugging the whole family as a way of getting attention suddenly shapes up when her parents treat her to the riding lessons she longs for. Or a husband and wife who have been on bad terms make a new start by having a "second honeymoon."

Sometimes merely coming to someone in a completely new way is enough to begin a positive trend. This happened to one young scientist working on a research and development project, whose boss ordered him to make a special client presentation on the subject. The young man refused, claiming this was premature, but his boss told him to do it or leave the company. When the scientist got over his anger, he wrote his boss an apologetic letter, in effect saying that he would join what he couldn't fight, and accept orders. In a flash his boss's mood changed; he took the younger man on an amicable plane trip and completely reversed his earlier decision.

A good technique for approaching someone differently is to ask advice. One engineer who had been at loggerheads with his boss for almost a year and would have been fired if he had not held patents which were valuable to the company, went to see his boss bearing a list of all the constructive projects he was working on and asked for the man's advice. His boss opened up like a flower, pulling out a drawer full of his own projects and talking for hours about his own business worries.

Asking for someone's advice should be done in a way that makes it as easy as possible for the other person to appear generous and knowledgeable. For example, a woman who is on bad terms with her mother can often undo the damage by asking her advice about the children. She will be still more successful if she encourages the older woman to talk out her own point of view and air her troubles.

Another way to plant a rose is to avert a danger for someone, and create a positive debt. During one of my previous jobs I was often asked to advise my boss during contract discussions with his attorney. I was frequently able to uncover points that were not in my boss's best interest. Looking shocked, he would get the attorney to change them, then ask me if I had any other suggestions. At this point it was easy to get a few changes made in my own favor.

Yet another rose is doing a good turn by taking over someone's chores. It could be doing the income-tax returns for your husband, cleaning the oven for your wife or taking the neighbor's kids for the weekend. The same technique works excellently in many business and professional situations when you feel your boss should give more substantial appreciation of your talents, like a raise or a promotion.

You simply expand your duties to include some of your boss's donkey-work, then request the job-title covering the additional duties, and finally ask for the money. Getting the raise will virtually assure you of another: not to get one would have sent you on the skids in many businesses where the harsh fact of life is that you either go up or out.

Here you have successfully pushed two important buttons. Under the principle of reciprocity, your boss will repay you by giving you the raise or promotion. He will also feel good about it, because his Angel complex will smooth the way by confirming his own rightness. It is a classic example of how almost any bad situation can be turned inside out to everyone's advantage.

PRINCIPLES

We can never make up other people's minds for them.

It is more natural for people to seek friends than enemies.

To reverse a bad situation, explain, make reparation or "plant a rose."

EXERCISES

1. Think over a painful fight you have had with someone. What did you do (if anything) to resolve the situation, and with what result? What would you do knowing what you know now?

2. If you are presently in any kind of bad human relations situation, what can you do to settle it?

3. Next time you meet a bad-tempered stranger, see if you can make him feel better for having talked briefly or smiled with you. Note your response to the initial grumpiness, and the response to your interest. To what means of communication did he most readily respond?

8

THE JOURNEY
TO ITHACA

"When you start on your journey to Ithaca,"
said the Greek poet C. P. Cavafy, "ask that the
way be long." Pray for a lifetime crammed
with sea smells and trading ports, with
"mother of pearl and corals, amber and ebony,
and pleasurable perfumes of all kinds," so
that you will arrive at your life's destination
old, perhaps, but laden with rich experiences.
Wisely, you will not expect your personal
Ithaca to have anything left to give you, but
"Ithaca has given you the splendid journey.

Without her you would never have taken
the road."

*The human spirit needs goals just as much as any
ship.* With no destination, both may go round
in circles forever. As captain, you must know
and be responsible for your course, and take
frequent compass checks to be sure you are
headed in the proper direction. Do *you* know
what your goals are, and if they are right for
you?

It is easy to get carried away by your Jehovah
complex, demand the impossible of yourself
and criticize yourself beyond reason. If your
target is impossible, you will not only be deaf
to the world, but hostile as well and end up
blaming other people for your dissatisfaction.
If you have no goals at all, you and your family
or business will do no better than a row boat
filled with people all pulling in different
directions.

Wherever your journey leads you, *it will only
be lastingly profitable if you are truly ethical in everything you undertake* and act in a way that will
affirm the lives of yourself and others to the

greatest degree. *Behind every code of ethics stands love*, beautifully defined by St. Paul in his Letter to the Corinthians.

Many people falter at this idea of love because they find it so hard to love themselves and believe they have nothing to give others. While you owe it to yourself to be physically and emotionally fit, loving yourself is not where love starts. Start first by loving and affirming life. Then, if you can, love your neighbor and all those nearest to you. Under the rule of reciprocity your love will be returned, making it possible for you to love yourself. As you act, so will you become. And your attitude of self-confidence almost anticipates the result. If you think you *can*, you are right, but if you think you *can't*, you are right again. Which is it to be?

Good human relations start at home, and they are a gift which must be shared. This is how John Donne explained it:

> No man is an island, entire of itself; every man is a piece of the continent, a part of the main. If a clod be washed away by the sea, Eu-

rope is the less, as well as if a promontory were,
as well as if a manor of thy friends were, or of
thine own were. Any man's death diminishes
me, because I am involved in mankind. And
therefore never send to know for whom the
bell tolls; it tolls for thee.

Where you are evil or destructive, other
lives may be driven to repay, adding to the
world's hurt. But in the end, they will reject
you, and your life's story will have been written on the wind.

When you love and affirm, *your act of loving
contributes to the eternity of others*; to the time-
lessness of their emotions, their grasping after
some kind of immortality, their rejection of the
imminence of death.

In this eternity, you can also find your own.
Every constructive thing you do will be wel-
comed, and the good people receive from you
will be repaid, either to you or to someone else
in their circle. Your name may or may not be
remembered, but insofar as your life has
affirmed life, it will remain a part of the actions
of others.

134

PRINCIPLES

We need goals which are realistic to our needs and subject to review at appropriate times.

To prosper, we must be ethical in everything we undertake.

To be ethical, we must love—life, our neighbor and then ourselves.

Every act of loving contributes to the eternity of both others and ourselves.

EXERCISES

1. Go over all the first exercises in Chapter 2. Re-evaluate:
   (a) what are your main goals in life, and are these right for you?
   (b) are you in good physical and emotional shape? Did you start that diet, exercise, stop smoking or whatever? (If not, do it!)

2. Make a definite plan for re-examining your goals at specified intervals, e.g. your birth-

day, New Year, etc., as well as when your mood or instinct advises you of the need for change.

3. Read the philosophies of the successful of the world—not those who are successful in terms of mere money or notoriety, but in their relationships with others.

4. What changes in your life and attitudes can you see after reading this book and doing the exercises? Cross check with your partner.

5. What changes would you still like to make? What plans have you made for doing this?

6. Last, read the book over again!

SUGGESTED READING

Stephen Vincent Benet, *The Devil and Daniel Webster*, Holt, Rinehart and Winston, New York, 1937.

Richard Nelson Bolles, *What Color Is Your Parachute?*, Ten Speed Press, Berkeley, 1972.

Richard Nelson Bolles, *The Three Boxes of Life*, Ten Speed Press, Berkeley, 1976.

Dale Carnegie, *How to Win Friends and Influence People*, Pocket Books, New York.

Russell Conwell, *Acres of Diamonds*, Pyramid Books, New York, 1966.

Jo Coudert, *Advice from a Failure*, Stein & Day, New York, 1965.

Eli Djeddah, *Moving Up*, Ten Speed Press, Berkeley, 1975.

Kahlil Gibran, *The Prophet*, Alfred Knopf, New York, 1973.

NOW THAT I KNOW WHICH SIDE IS UP

Bernard Haldane, *How to Make a Habit of Success*, Unity
   Books, 1966.
Laura Huxley, *Your Are Not The Target*, Farrar, Straus &
   Giroux, New York, 1963.
Carl Jung, *Psychological Types*, Harcourt, Brace & Co.
   Inc. 1923.
Maxwell Maltz, *Psycho-Cybernetics*, Prentice-Hall,
   Englewood Cliffs, N.J., 1960.
Joseph Banks Rhine, *Extra-Sensory Perception*, B. Hum-
   phries, Boston, 1964.
Albert Schweitzer, *Reverence for Life*, Harper & Row,
   New York, 1969.